I0808036

HELP!

SHE'S STRUGGLING WITH PORNOGRAPHY

Rachel Coyle

Consulting Editor: Dr. Paul Tautges

ISBN
Paper: 978-1-63342-033-5
epub: 978-1-63342-034-2
Kindle: 978-1-63342-035-9

Published by **Shepherd Press**
P.O. Box 24
Wapwallopen, PA 18660

www.shepherdpress.com

All Scripture quotations, unless stated otherwise, are from the New American Standard Bible, The Lockman Foundation, 1995.

Printed in Colombia

Designed by **documen**

Contents

Introduction

While strolling through the aisles of a local chain store, Kate suddenly felt a strong urge for a chocolate candy bar. Her craving was so powerful that she forgot what she was shopping for and headed to the candy aisle. "I must *satisfy this desire," Kate silently told herself. Her stomach ached for something sweet as she searched the rows and rows of options, wondering what would satisfy her mounting hunger. Suddenly, she spotted something she had never tasted before. "Great New Taste!" the label announced. "Satisfaction Guaranteed!" it promised. "No More Hunger Cravings!" it claimed. "That's the one I must have," Kate convinced herself.*

Hastily, Kate grabbed the candy bar and tore off the wrapper, telling herself she would pay for it later. She felt out of control, unable to wait any longer to satisfy her desire. The candy bar looked delicious and pleasing to the eye. A rich chocolate shell, coated chewy caramel, and almonds blended in soft chocolate nougat. Kate bit off a large chunk and slowly chewed the candy, thinking only about how good it tasted. All her senses were captivated by the chocolate candy bar. It seemed so gratifying that she convinced herself she would never need any more candy again after finishing this one.

Kate soon noticed a strange, unexpected texture in her mouth. Instead of eating almonds, she found she was chomping on gritty gravel. Her throat became parched as an intense thirst strangled her. The caramel and chocolate nougat fell apart in her mouth as they turned into thick mud. The taste was unbearable! Her throat closed off and her stomach churned at the thought of what could be in the mud—in her very own mouth. Shocked by the sudden realization that what she had enjoyed for a moment was actually filthy mud and grit covered in a chocolate candy shell, she spewed it out of her mouth and onto the floor, right there in the middle of the store. Humiliated, she gagged and coughed while frantically searching for water to remove the rancid taste.

After a long moment at the water fountain, the atrocious flavor cleared away. Kate glanced down at the remainder of the bar still in her hand. Her thoughts turned to how good that first bite had tasted ... and she longed for more.

This is the way pornography operates. It is sin covered in an appealing package. The "candy coating" deceives you into believing that pornography will deliver what it promises: satisfaction, happiness, a thrill, or whatever you are looking for at the time. And, at first, it seems to deliver what it promises. But the pleasures of sin are short-lived (Hebrews 11:25). In time, your attitude toward pornography develops into a love–hate relationship: you realize it does not give full satisfaction, yet you crave more.

No New Problem

Ecclesiastes 1:9 tells us that "there is nothing new under the sun." Sexual sin is nothing new. However, it seems rampant in our culture. Many Hollywood movies or current television shows make light of preserving sex for marriage. Secular musicians write graphic songs about sex. Innuendoes and seductively dressed actors and actresses appear in commercials selling everything from hamburgers to cars. Nearly every women's magazine features articles about sex. Scantily-clad men and women are plastered on billboards and magazine covers—and the list goes on. It seems that we cannot get away from this issue; sex dominates our society. Therefore, it is no surprise that pornography is an increasing problem.

For years, pornography was assumed to be a problem that only men struggle against. The subject is taboo among many Christians today—especially women. It is rare to hear a preacher or speaker refer to pornography as a problem that women struggle with *as well as* men. While some of the particular details of the battle differ for women and men, women can *and do* become enslaved to pornography, even in Christian circles. Whether we avoid this issue because of ignorance or fear, the reality is that many women are embarrassed, fearful, and unsure of where to turn for help. The following are true stories of three women whom I call Denise, Michelle, and Heather.[1]

In the Real World

Denise had been a Christian for a couple of years when she approached me for discipleship. We began meeting together weekly to discuss Bible study and application. Over the course of several weeks, Denise opened up the darkest secret of her heart in a desperate plea for help: she was in

1 These are pseudonyms for actual counselees of mine.

bondage to pornography. It had been going on for over ten years. Was there any hope for complete freedom? Did she just have to learn how to "cope" with her problem? Denise needed hope and help, and she had come to me for both.

Michelle struggled too. She confided in me about her on-off involvement with pornography that had gone on for more than a decade. She started looking at pornography during college with her friends. A few years later she heard the gospel and placed her faith in Jesus Christ, but that did not mean instant freedom in her case. She no longer sought out videos, but impure memories were triggered when a movie, article, or book suggested anything sexual. Even "clean" romantic comedies or television shows brought back a flood of memories, sending her mind down a hazardous road. She continued to struggle with pornography's common counterpart: masturbation. She was given some inadequate counsel by a well-meaning friend: just pray for freedom and claim it. Michelle tried, but it wasn't enough. The struggle continued.

Heather also came to me for counseling, trusting me enough to share how deeply enslaved to pornography she had become. She had been secretly struggling for years. For her, it had digressed to more perverted and hazardous sexual sins. Pornography had become such a part of her life that it was painful to even consider giving it up. And yet she wanted to for the sake of obedience to Jesus Christ.

Can you relate to any of these women? Or do you know a woman who can? Perhaps you still doubt that pornography is an issue for women. Here are some statistics for those who find numbers more convincing.

Top Ten Reviews, a research organization, has conducted research concerning Internet pornography. Here are their statistics concerning women:

» 13% of women (surveyed) admit to accessing pornography at work

» 17% of all women struggle with pornography addiction

» 1 in 3 visitors to all adult (pornographic) websites are women

» 9.4 million women access adult (pornographic) websites each *month*[2]

2 "Internet Pornography Statistics," at: www.toptenreviews.com; accessed August 1, 2010.

Setting Captives Free is a ministry that provides biblical help for men and women who want to be free from pornography and other sexual sins.[3] Because this is a biblically-based program, the majority of men and women enrolled are churchgoers. As of February 2004, 3,535 women were enrolled in the program, forming 13 percent of the ministry's total enrollment. Three years later, 7,653 women were enrolled in the same course.[4] In just three years, the number of *women* seeking help more than doubled! If over 7,000 women *in our churches* are currently seeking freedom from sexual sin (including, but not limited to, pornography), the number of women living with this secret might astound us.

As you read this minibook, where do you find yourself in all this? Are you curious about pornography? Do you indulge in it? Maybe you are the woman that others seek out for help. Think about where you are, where you want to be, and what you hope the wonderful counselor Jesus will teach you through his Word, the Bible, as we learn together.

3 More information, visit: www.settingcaptivesfree.com.

4 From email correspondence with Jodi White, Mentor at Setting Captives Free, on February 18, 2004 and February 7, 2007.

1 What Is Pornography?

Most people assume that pornography consists of visual images—pictures or movies portraying some form of sensuality or sexual act. The truth is that it exists in many forms; we must not limit it to visual images.

Defining Pornography

Consider Webster's Dictionary definition of pornography: "Obscene writings, drawings, photographs, or the like, especially those having little or no artistic merit."[5] Merriam-Webster provides a more thorough definition: "1) the depiction of erotic behavior (as in pictures or writings) intended to cause sexual excitement ... 3) the depiction of acts in a sensational manner so as to arouse a quick intense emotional reaction."[6]

5 "Pornography," *Webster's Encyclopedic Unabridged Dictionary of the English Language* (San Diego: Thunder Bay Press, 2001), 1506.

6 "Pornography," Merriam-Webster online dictionary, at: www.merriam-webster.com.

These definitions force us out of the "box" we typically put pornography into. Pornography includes *any* representation of sensual or erotic behavior. This is how I define it: "Writings, literature, magazine articles, books, billboards, drawings, photographs, Internet images, movies, television, *and things like these* that portray, describe, or visually show sensual material or sexual acts, often resulting in sexual arousal." Need I be more specific?

Pornography for Women

As women, things that entertain our imaginations attract us. Soap operas, romance books, television, movies, and magazine articles appeal to women. They tantalize our minds, conjure up secret fantasies, and ultimately influence our emotions. Unlike men, a woman's sexual arousal is primarily connected to our feelings and emotions rather than sight. To overcome bondage to pornography, a woman has to be wary of *anything* that influences her emotions in such a way that she becomes sexually aroused. (That influence is reserved for her husband alone.)

Images

We all know that images can be pornographic. Visual erotic images are readily available, even in our own homes, via television, magazines, catalogs, and the Internet. They are plastered all over the streets and highways of the world on billboards. Seductive pictures are not difficult to come by.

Movies

Pornographic movies are also readily available. Some stores specialize in erotic movies, but you can browse your local video rental store and find them in the midst of family-friendly films. And for those who would never rent a video, there's pay-per-view television, the Internet, and even cell phones.

Today, many movies rated PG-13 and R in the United States contain highly suggestive or downright graphic sexual scenes. In the United Kingdom, films rated 15 often have explicit sexual content; even some 12-rated films contain significant sexual content. Regardless of the rating, even sexual innuendoes can generate impure images in the mind's eye. Sexual scenes and innuendoes in movies can be an immense obstacle for women.

Television

A number of television shows and commercials flash sexually charged images into our homes. They are filled with innuendoes and nearly-naked men and women, which can trigger improper thoughts or desires. And then there are soap operas, a socially acceptable format for women. Soaps regularly include simulated scenes of sexual acts, which puts them in the category of soft-core pornography.[7] Other television programs, including popular sitcoms, promote pornography in their episodes by making positive comments or jokes about it.[8]

Please beware: What we allow into our minds will affect our thoughts and judgments. When we fill our minds with the toxins of soap operas and sexually charged television shows, they *will* influence our perspective of sex and may weaken our consciences to the dangers of pornography.

Internet

This is the vehicle of choice by many people

7 "Soft-core," Merriam-Webster online dictionary. See also "Pornography" at www.answers.com.

8 Popular sitcom *Friends* features an episode entitled "The One with the Free Porn" (1998) (episode list at Internet Movie Database, www.imdb.com).

today, including women. Through the Internet, we have access to everything, from images to personal contacts, just with a click of the mouse. The convenience and impression of privacy the Internet offers makes it easier for women to indulge in any form of pornography.

Books

Erotic literature is pornography. Erotic romance novels can arouse us to the point of desire for sexual release. Steamy novels enable us to escape into a fantasy world, drawing up graphic pictures in our minds. This is one of the most prominent yet most acceptable formats for women.

Magazine Articles

Over forty years ago, *Cosmopolitan* was tagged as "the woman's *Playboy*"—not because of pictures, but because of its sexually charged articles.[9] Imagine how much more shameless this magazine is today. You don't have to pick up a *Cosmo* to find pornography these days. Sex articles smear the pages of many magazines, covers feature men and women *au naturel*, with similar

9 *Technical Report of the Commission on Obscenity and Pornography*, vol. 3, *The Marketplace, The Industry* (Washington, DC: US Government Printing Office, 1971), 85.

images splashing the pages inside, and even article *titles* openly address sexual issues in a distasteful manner.

Music

When you hear music, do you really *listen* to the words? Some of the music today is pornography for the mind. If you pay attention to the music resounding through the speakers at the mall or your gym, you may hear musicians use explicit language to depict sensual acts. Others are more covert, merely implying the theme of sex. Music is particularly powerful (and potentially dangerous) for women.[10]

Pornography's Common Counterpart: Masturbation

I would be remiss if I did not address the issue of masturbation. Some women indulge in masturbation apart from pornography; others use pornography and do not masturbate. But the two usually accompany each other. You may think, "I enjoy romance novels but I don't masturbate or

10 Patricia Schiller, "Effects of Mass Media on the Sexual Behavior of Adolescent Females," in *Technical Report*, vol. 1, *Preliminary Studies*, 191-195.

anything." Beware, because it is often the next stage in a progression from pornography. And when masturbation produces a high, it is like fastening a padlock on the chains of sin: it is the surest way to bondage.

Webster's defines masturbation as "the stimulation or manipulation of one's own genitals, especially to orgasm; sexual self-gratification."[11] Is it sinful? There are differing views on this subject. Unfortunately, we cannot look up the word *masturbation* in a Bible concordance and find a list of verses about it. We have to consider the biblical principles surrounding this issue. Here are three reasons I believe masturbation is sinful.

Masturbation Is Selfish

The motive of masturbation is to please oneself. It is possible to engage in the act and even experience arousal apart from lustful fantasies; sometimes Michelle would masturbate out of sheer boredom. She could stimulate herself without fantasizing, reading, or looking at pornography. But this was still a *self*-centered act of *self*-gratification: she was completely focused on pleasing herself. Scripture advises us,

11 Webster's, 1184.

> ... *whatever you do,* do all to the glory of God.
>
> (1 Corinthians 10:31b, emphasis added)

Can a self-centered act truly be done to God's glory?

Masturbation Encourages Impure Thoughts

Sexual fantasies or images almost always accompany masturbation. Using pornography can make you want to masturbate for sexual release. Philippians 4:8 instructs,

> *Finally, brethren, whatever is true ... honorable ... right ...* pure *... lovely ... of good repute, if there is any excellence and if anything worthy of praise, dwell on these things.*

If a thought does not pass the "Philippians 4:8 Test," it does not belong in your mind.

Masturbation Easily Enslaves

I have reserved the most important point for last. Even if you do not agree with my first two objections, I plead with you to consider this one. I have already said that the high that masturbation produces is like putting a padlock on the chains of sin. The act feeds the desires of the flesh, which God strongly warns us against:

> *For the mind set on the flesh is death, but the mind set on the Spirit is life and peace, because the mind set on the flesh is hostile toward God; for it does not subject itself to the law of God, for it is not even able to do so, and those who are in the flesh cannot please God.*
>
> *(Romans 8:6–8)*

The more we feed the flesh, the hungrier it becomes. Ultimately, we become slaves to our flesh. Proverbs 5:22 describes the entrapping capacity of sin:

> *His own iniquities will capture*
> *the wicked,*
> *And he will be held with the cords of his*
> *sin.*

Masturbation will capture you and wrap you in its chains. Your flesh—your desire for physical pleasure—becomes consuming and powerful. You eventually feel overcome by it. Listen to the instruction from Romans 6:

> *... and do not go on presenting the members of your body to sin as instruments of unrighteousness ... For sin shall not be master over you, for you are not under law but under grace.*
>
> (vv. 13–14)

If you choose to masturbate, sin will eventually master you.[12]

12 For more information, see articles on masturbation at www.settingcaptivesfree.com.

2 Understanding Addiction

There is a dangerous predicament today: We do not know where to look in God's Word for the solutions to our problems. This is often because we use non-biblical words to describe problems and struggles. It is not wrong or sinful to use words such as "addiction," but it does pose some potential problems.

When we do not use biblical terms to define our struggles, it is easy to think the Bible is not adequate to address all the problems of life. We find ourselves turning elsewhere for solutions to sin. Let's get back to the Bible and develop the skill of biblically defining the problems with which we struggle.

Identify the biblical terms that describe sexual addiction in the following passages:

> *For just as you presented your members as slaves to impurity and to lawlessness, resulting in further lawlessness, so*

> *now present your members as slaves to righteousness ...*
>
> (Romans 6:19b)

> *Therefore consider the members of your earthly body as dead to immorality, impurity, passion, evil desire, and greed, which amounts to idolatry.*
>
> (Colossians 3:5)

> *... [B]y what a man is overcome, by this he is enslaved.*
>
> (2 Peter 2:19b)

God addresses sexual addiction in terms of *slavery* to sin and *idolatry*. Repeatedly using pornography and/or engaging in masturbation—whether every day or once in a while—is idolatry and slavery to sin (see Romans 6:12–13; 16). If you want a more adequate understanding of this addiction and how to overcome it, look at what the Bible says about slavery to sin and idolatry.[13]

If this sounds a bit harsh, consider that labeling our sin problems as they really are gives us hope.

13 You can use a Bible concordance to look up the words "slavery" and "idolatry," or visit www.biblegateway.com and conduct a Bible search online.

We can repent from sin and be forgiven by the Lord Jesus Christ; he can set us *free* from sin (John 8:34–36; Romans 8:2). The alternative to forgiveness and freedom from sin is a life of "coping" with the addiction. If you are enslaved to pornography, don't settle for anything less than God's offer to you of complete forgiveness and lasting freedom.

Addiction Redefined as Slavery to Sin

Every one of us is born as a slave to sin:

> *... [W]hen you did not know God, you were slaves to those which by nature are no gods.*
>
> *(Galatians 4:8)*

We are not inherently good. We are inherently sinful. We come into this world separated from God, being dead in our sins (Ephesians 2:1). Praise God that Jesus Christ can set us free from slavery to sin and make us servants of righteousness and children of God (Romans 6:16–18).

But freedom from slavery to sin does not mean we will never sin again. Even believers in Christ continue to battle the flesh—indwelling sin. This is why the apostle Paul penned these words:

> *... [W]alk by the Spirit, and you will not carry out the desire of the flesh. For the flesh sets its desire against the Spirit, and the Spirit against the flesh; for these are in opposition to one another, so that you may not do the things that you please.*
>
> *(Galatians 5:16–17)*

By nature, sin enslaves. Hebrews 12:1 says that it "easily entangles us." By our choices and habits, we can even put ourselves in bondage to particular sins ("sins," not "sin" in the general sense, as we are born in bondage to sin). Forming a habit of any sin—from complaining to lying or pornography—leads us into bondage to that sin. Remember 2 Peter 2:19b: "... by what a man is overcome, by this he is enslaved." When you are overcome by a particular sin, you are enslaved to it. Pornography and masturbation both have the capacity to overcome your mind and body so that you find yourself thinking about it anytime, anywhere. You plan it, plot it, and pursue it. And this happens again ... and again. You can almost feel the weight of steel chains around your mind and your body! This is slavery.

Addiction Redefined as Idolatry

What do you think of when you hear the word "idolatry"? Bowing before wooden objects or clay statues? Actually, idolatry is an issue for all of us. A key passage on this subject is Ezekiel 14:1–11. I encourage you to find a Bible and read through the whole passage. Notice from the following verses what God says about the residence, result, and his requirement concerning idolatry:

» The *residence* of idolatry: the heart. "[T]hese men have set up their idols in their hearts and have put right before their faces the stumbling block of their iniquity" (v. 3; see also v. 7).

» The *result* of idolatry: separation from God. "[T]he hearts of the house of Israel ... are estranged from Me through all their idols"; "... anyone ... who separates himself from Me ..." (vv. 5, 7).

» God's *requirement*: repentance. "Repent and turn away from your idols and turn your faces away from all your abominations" (v. 6).

We all have the tendency to give other people, or things, God's rightful place. We worship something other than God, thus committing idolatry that only he sees. Idols of the heart are formed when we do not heed the instruction in Hebrews 12:1 to "lay aside every encumbrance and the sin which so easily entangles us," but put those stumbling blocks right in front of us instead. "Addictions" are good indicators that heart idolatry is going on. One definition of "addicted" is: "*devoted* or *given up to* a practice or habit ..." (emphasis mine).[14] That sounds like worship to me!

Involvement with pornography is the fruit of an idolatrous heart. There is something you want *more* than pleasing the Lord Jesus and honoring him, something you want *more* than being content with what God has (or has not) given to you. I want to address just two idols often at the heart of pornography: *physical pleasure* and *easy, pain-free living*. Certainly, if you are struggling with pornography, these are not the only idols that may be operating in your own life, but I doubt that you will *not* find these at work.

The Idol of Physical Pleasure

One very common reason why pornography and masturbation captivate women is simply

---

14 *Webster's*, 23.

the feeling the two produce.[15] This was true for Michelle, Heather, and Denise. They wanted to experience a similar high to the physiological high produced by drugs in a person's body. In this case, the idol is physical pleasure; they were willing to sin in order to achieve a physical high.

The Idol of Easy or Pain-Free Living

Pornography enables us to escape from reality into a fantasy world. It can become a refuge from difficulties or disappointments in life. Anything from the burden of having to clean a dirty house to the despair of a broken relationship can send a woman running to this unreliable refuge. Indulging in pornography can become a way of avoiding undesirable responsibilities.

There is Hope for Freedom

When we label problems and struggles biblically, we realize that God provides the solutions. Pornography and masturbation are biblically addressed in terms of slavery to sin and idolatry. Praise God

15 Mike Cleveland, *Pure Freedom* (Bemidji, MN: Focus, 2002), testimony on p. 96; conversation with Doug Weiss, licensed psychologist, March 18, 2004; and interviews with Michelle, Denise, and Heather (counselees), Belleair, FL, May 2004.

that he has provided a way for us to be free from bondage to sin and from the worship of idols! It starts with repentance and faith in Jesus Christ. In the next chapter we will look more closely at what God provides for us so that we can have victory over sin.

3 God's Provisions for Victory

Heather, Denise, and Michelle all chose to believe that God would give them everything they needed to have victory over sin. They did not want to live in slavery to pornography any longer; they were not satisfied with "coping." These women chose to take hold of God's provisions for victory, and he set them *free*. The same choice lies before any other woman who is enslaved to pornography today.

The Lord Jesus Christ

> *The night is almost gone, and the day is near. Therefore let us lay aside the deeds of darkness and put on the armor of light ... But put on the Lord Jesus Christ, and make no provision for the flesh in regard to its lusts.*
>
> (Romans 13:12; 14)

Pornography is a deed of darkness. We need to

bring it into the light and "put on the Lord Jesus Christ," which has two practical implications: salvation and sanctification. Let me explain these terms.

Salvation

Every person longs for affirmation, acceptance, and love. But we have a genuine *need* that transcends these longings: the need for *forgiveness of sin*. Just as a lawbreaker deserves a penalty, so sin deserves punishment. The book of Romans tells us "all have sinned" and that "the wages of sin is death" (3:23; 6:23). We would never expect an impartial judge in the court of law to declare a guilty lawbreaker to be innocent. Likewise, as a holy and just Judge, God will not simply excuse our sins. But because God is loving, merciful, and gracious, he provided his Son to receive the punishment for our sins (Hebrews 2:17; 1 John 2:1–2; 4:9–10). Jesus paid our fine (death) so that we can be forgiven. "[W]ithout shedding of blood there is no forgiveness" (Hebrews 9:22b). Jesus is called "the Lamb of God, who takes away the sin of the world!" (John 1:29). I can't summarize this any better than Scripture:

> *For Christ also died for sins once for all,*

the just for the unjust, so that He might bring us to God.

(1 Peter 3:18)

Jesus' life didn't end in the grave. He conquered sin and death when God raised him from the dead three days after the crucifixion (1 Corinthians 15). The gift of salvation—forgiveness of sins and eternal life in heaven—is available for everyone through Jesus Christ (John 14:6; Romans 10:9–10). The moment we repent of sin and trust in Jesus, he saves us from the penalty of sin (hell) and the power of sin in our life on earth. We are "clothed" with his righteousness, his perfection, and we are called children of God (John 1:12–13; Romans 8:8–14; Galatians 2:17; Philippians 3:9).

Have you acknowledged that you are a sinner? Not just because you might be struggling with a sin like pornography, but because every one of us is born a sinner. We *will* stand before God one day, guilty and facing the "death penalty" in a place called hell—unless we repent and trust in the sacrifice that Jesus Christ made on our behalf. Have you done this?

Salvation is the first step toward victory over pornography. A woman battling pornography must be certain that she is a child of God through faith in the Lord Jesus Christ. Only then does she have the capacity to move any further in the battle for her purity. Apart from Christ, we may be able to change our behavior for a while, but only Jesus transforms our hearts. A woman will not be free from pornography and all its roots embedded in her heart until she has faith in Jesus Christ.

True faith in Christ yields the fruit of righteousness. This is called sanctification.

Sanctification

The moment we are saved, not only are we forgiven of sin and freed from the *penalty* of sin upon physical death, we are also free from the *power* of sin during this life on earth (Romans 6:14–22). In Christ, we have the power to reject sin—including pornography and masturbation.

This is not to say that a Christian cannot struggle with these sins, but it is just that: a *struggle*. Christians can battle any kind of sin because our sinful flesh does not simply vanish when we are saved. When we yield our lives to Jesus Christ, the battle is on! We are no longer allies of our flesh, but enemies against it (Romans 7–8; Ephesians 6:12). When the lusts of our flesh come on strong, we now have the ability—because of Christ in us—to put off those desires and replace them with the thoughts, desires, and actions of the Lord Jesus. This lifelong process is called "progressive sanctification."

Progressive Sanctification

We can think of progressive sanctification as "becoming like Jesus Christ." Ephesians 4:22–24 sums up this process:

> *... [I]n reference to your former manner of life ... lay aside the old self, which is being corrupted in accordance with the lusts of deceit, and ... be renewed in the spirit of your mind, and put on the new self, which in the likeness of God has been created in righteousness and holiness of the truth.*

Lasting change happens gradually. God calls us to patience and perseverance as we put off our old ways of living, renew our minds, and put on new life habits.

How many habits have you been unsuccessful at breaking? Perhaps it is because God's Word teaches us to *replace* bad habits with righteous ones. If a woman tries to stop using pornography without replacing her sinful thoughts, actions, and desires with good ones, she will return to pornography again.

Michelle learned this painful truth. I explained earlier that she was told that if she confessed her sin of pornography to God, she would be free. The woman in whom Michelle confided had good intentions, but she was wrong. Confession is the *first* step, not the *only* step toward freedom. Michelle willingly confessed and asked for God's forgiveness. However, although she was determined to stop, Michelle was not actively renewing her mind with God's Word. She had never considered replacing her sinful longings with those that please God, nor did she know how to do this. She thought that she was "cured" when she confessed her sin. As a result, she became deeply discouraged when she relapsed into her sinful habit.

Many of us focus on simply breaking bad habits, rather than replacing them with good ones. But the way to freedom is to put off sin, renew our minds, and then replace sin with righteous behavior. This is not behavior modification. Renewing our minds involves transforming our thoughts, beliefs, perspectives, attitudes, and even desires, so that they line up with what God wants for us (according to his Word). This is done by faith, not based on how we feel. We choose to filter our thoughts through God's Word. We relinquish worldly perspectives to his righteous ones. We decide to believe the Bible in spite of our feelings. We submit our attitudes and our very desires in obedience to him. (Again, this is a daily, sometimes moment-by-moment, process.) Such a profound renewal of the mind accompanied by a change in our actions is true repentance.

Repentance Yields Sanctification

Genuine change (putting off the old/putting on the new) is the outgrowth of repentance. Repentance involves a deep hatred of sin, so much so that we are willing to turn away from it even though it may be painful.

> *He who conceals his transgressions will*
> *not prosper,*
> *But he who* confesses and forsakes *them*
> *will find compassion.*
> (Proverbs 28:13, emphasis added)

If you are enslaved by pornography, are you ready and willing to do *whatever it takes* to be free from its chains? If not, pray! Ask God to grant you the gift of repentance from sin (see 2 Timothy 2:25).

Ask for a glimpse of his holiness, so that you see your sin for what it is and the price Jesus paid so you could be forgiven and set free.

Do Whatever It Takes

It will take some drastic measures—some radical decisions—for a woman to overcome this sin. After explaining that adultery begins in the heart, Jesus gave this instruction:

> *If your right eye makes you stumble, tear it out and throw it from you; for it is better for you to lose one of the parts of your body, than for your whole body to be thrown into hell. If your right hand makes you stumble, cut it off and throw it from you; for it is better for you to lose one of the parts of your body, than for your whole body to go into hell.*
>
> (Matthew 5:29–30)

These instructions are an intentional exaggeration; a woman who is blind and lame still has the ability to commit adultery in her heart. Jesus' shocking illustration teaches that overcoming sexual sin requires extreme measures. We have to radically "cut off" whatever causes us to sin. Do whatever it takes to remove the hindrances, and build a hedge of protection around yourself. Prepare to make some drastic decisions.

If you are tempted to look at pornography or fantasize while watching TV, cancel cable or unplug the set (maybe even put the TV set away for a time). If a particular billboard or pornographic store is a temptation, change your driving route. If you are tempted by the Internet, cut off your Internet access from home, put a strong block on it, or implement some form of Internet accountability, such as Covenant Eyes.[16] If romance novels entice you, destroy them. Prayerfully consider the sources of temptation in your life. Write out how you will "cut them off" as much as possible. Take drastic measures for Jesus' sake; consider the drastic measures he took for you.

Obviously, there are some things you cannot control. Don't set yourself up for failure or make an excuse to sin with thoughts like, "I can't change anything" or "I know I'm going to mess up so I might as well ..." Instead, be confident that God will provide a way out so you do not have to sin. Commit this verse to memory:

---

16 For more information, visit www.covenanteyes.com.

> *No temptation has overtaken you but such as is common to man; and God is faithful, who will not allow you to be tempted beyond what you are able, but with the temptation will provide the way of escape also, so that you will be able to endure it.*
>
> *(1 Corinthians 10:13)*

Look for the "way of escape" that God provides for you during tempting times.

Denise had to stay in a hotel room during a week-long business trip—a circumstance that was out of her control. There she had access to cable TV. She shared a room with a co-worker, so she nonchalantly asked the woman (another Christian) to keep the remote control. Denise didn't divulge the details behind this action; she simply chose not to touch the remote control. If Denise had been alone in the hotel room, she could have unplugged the TV or removed the batteries from the remote control and given them to a staff member at the front desk. The most extreme measure, but perhaps necessary for Denise, would have been to remove the TV from her hotel room altogether. Overcoming sin requires drastic action at times. If you love Jesus

Christ more than your sin, you will have the courage to do whatever it takes.

Overcoming our sin is a painful process. At times, we may feel as if we are cutting off our right hand or tearing out our eye! Remember that Jesus Christ defeated the power of sin for all who believe on him; that includes *you*. You, or the woman you may be counseling, *can* have victory over this gripping sin, no matter how intense is sin's grasp or the pain of cutting it off (see Ephesians 6:10–18; James 4:7). Our obedience to the Lord will reap many blessings that cannot compare to what we leave behind.

The Holy Spirit

God has not left us to fend for ourselves as we strive against sin. He has given us the Holy Spirit (John 14:16–17). The Holy Spirit is our Comforter and Helper, exactly what you need if you are striving to overcome bondage to pornography. The Spirit will console you, encourage you, teach you, and help you to change.

The Holy Spirit guides Christians into the truth by using God's instrument of truth: the Bible (Psalm 119:160; John 17:17). Learning and believing the truth is imperative to overcoming idolatry, since idolatry is saturated with lies. It is time to replace the lies you have believed with the truth of God.

The Word of God

Psalm 119:9–11 addresses the question, "How can a young man keep his way pure?" It answers,

> *By keeping it according to Your word.*
> *With all my heart I have sought You;*
> *Do not let me wander from Your*
> *commandments.*
> *Your word I have treasured in my heart,*
> *That I may not sin against You.*

This passage reveals the secret to leading a pure life: living according to the Word of God. We renew our minds through the truth of God's Word. Obeying the Bible protects us from sin.

God's Word is necessary (we *need* it) and sufficient (it is *enough*) to teach us how to have victory over any sin. The Word is living, active, and powerful. It alone has the ability to reveal the thoughts and intentions of our hearts (Hebrews 4:12).

> *All Scripture is inspired by God and profitable for teaching, for reproof, for correction, for training in righteousness;*

> *so that the man of God may be adequate, equipped for* every *good work.*
>
> (2 *Timothy* 3:16–17, emphasis added)

The Bible must have a place of priority in our lives. It is through the Bible that God speaks to us. It is our manual for living, not merely a history book or love letter from God. In the Bible are God's words for life—our daily bread (Deuteronomy 8:3; Matthew 4:4). The Word teaches us how to live. It reveals God to us and gives us life. We are saved by grace through faith alone, but true faith in Jesus Christ means that we bow the knee before our Lord and yield our lives to him. Just as a child shows love to a parent through obedience, so those who truly love God will obey him:

> *For this is the love of God, that we keep His commandments; and His commandments are not burdensome.*
>
> (1 John 5:3; compare 2:3)

Obedience produces blessing. The path of obedience is the way to true happiness.

Prayer

God speaks to us through his Word; we speak to

him through prayer. The Lord wants us to pour out our hearts before him. Through prayer we can confess our sins to God, and he responds by forgiving and cleansing us (1 John 1:9).

Genuine confession is not lip service. When it comes to prayer, God is more concerned with our hearts than he is with our words. The Old Testament tells us about David, described as being a man after God's own heart (1 Samuel 13:14). Yet David was not perfect; among other things, he made a devastating choice to commit adultery. God sent a prophet to confront David about his sin, and David's prayer of repentance is recorded for us in Psalm 51. Look at what we can learn from just a portion of that psalm:

» *Humility:* "Be gracious to me, O God, according to Your lovingkindness; according to the greatness of Your compassion blot out my transgressions. Wash me thoroughly from my iniquity and cleanse me from my sin. For I know my transgressions, and my sin is ever before me. Against You, You only, I have sinned ..." (vv. 1–4a). What humility! Genuine confession flows from a heart that is humble before God. David realized the depth of his sin and he longed for cleansing. Do you?

- » *Repentance:* "Create in me a clean heart, O God, and renew a steadfast spirit within me … Restore to me the joy of Your salvation and sustain me with a willing spirit. Then I will teach transgressors Your ways, and sinners will be converted to You … O Lord, open my lips, that my mouth may declare Your praise" (vv. 10, 12–13, 15). David repented and wanted God to change him. He asked for a clean heart and a renewed spirit that was steadfast—unwavering, resolved, loyal to the Lord. He asked the Lord for joy, and was determined to share it with others. Have you?
- » *Brokenness:* "The sacrifices of God are a broken spirit; a broken and a contrite heart, O God, You will not despise" (v. 17). Have you come to God in prayer with a broken and contrite (repentant) heart? This is the junction where sin ends and freedom begins. If your spirit is not broken and your heart not ready for repentance, plead with God to grant it to you. Then you will be ready to purge your heart of the roots of pornography and cultivate a heart of purity, a heart fully his.

4 Cultivating Christlikeness

Have you ever tried to pull weeds from a garden? I know well the frustration of spending hours pulling weeds, only later to learn that I neglected to pull the *roots* out. The nasty weeds cropped up again after a good drink of rain. After learning my lesson, one time, I sat in the dirt for hours in the hot sun, pulling up the weeds before planting our beautiful bushes. I wanted to do it right. Some of those weeds must have been four feet long! I kept pulling and pulling, careful not to yank too hard and sever the root. I wanted to *extract* the weed—pull the whole thing out of the dirt so I could grow a beautiful garden that wouldn't be choked out by the weeds sprouting up again.

This illustrates the importance of attacking sin at the *root*. The root of sin is always a matter of the heart. The heart is the "inner person" from which all the issues of life flow (Proverbs 4:23). Today's society tends to equate the heart with our emotions. According to God's Word, however, that is far too narrow a description of our hearts. Biblically speaking, the heart consists of our thoughts, attitudes, beliefs, desires, and choices (see Psalm 37:4; 73:7; Proverbs 15:28, 16:1; Jeremiah 12:3; Luke 9:47). God wants us to continually examine these and bring them into line with his Word and his ways.

Because sin is rooted in the heart, it is not enough simply to change our behavior. Whether we struggle with gossip, anger, cheating, discontentment, or pornography, we must deal with the problem at the heart level. We may be able to clean up our act, stop using pornography for a time, or put an end to masturbation. But if we do not address the issues of our hearts—the issues that have motivated us to continue with our sin in the first place—the change will not last; it is not a change that pleases God. The roots of our sin will yield the crop of another sort of weed. Maybe it will not be pornography again, but perhaps we will indulge in food. Or shopping. Or alcohol. The list goes on. We must not allow that to happen! We must do what Jesus taught us: attack our sin at the heart level.

> *For out of the heart come evil thoughts, murders, adulteries, fornications, thefts,*

false witness, slanders.

(Matthew 15:19)

If you are gripped by pornography, it is vital that you understand what you are seeking from it. What do you want from it? What do you get from it that keeps you going back for more? If those root issues are not dealt with, they will manifest themselves in other ways.

Ask the Lord to reveal how the following issues may be a part of your struggle. Seek his grace and help to extract the roots of sin from the soil of your heart, making it soft and ready to receive the Word and bear good fruit. Believe that he will give this help!

Cultivate Purity

The imaginations of our mind's eyes are as influential as images we see with our physical eyes. In Matthew 5:27–28, the Lord Jesus teaches that the physical eye *and* the mind's eye can cause us to sin:

You have heard that it was said, "You shall not commit adultery"; but I say to you that everyone who looks at a woman

> *with lust for her has already committed adultery with her in his heart.*

The Lord is teaching us a vital principle here: according to God, adultery is not limited to a physical act. We can commit adultery of the heart—through the impure thoughts of our mind's eyes—without physically acting upon those thoughts. This has significant application to pornography. To look upon a man who is not your husband, whether imagined or real, with sexual desire for him, is to commit adultery in your heart.

In order to be free from bondage to this sin, you should practice taking your mind captive to the obedience of Christ rather than being held captive by your mind (see 2 Corinthians 10:5). You may not be able to stop images from popping into your mind, but you can keep from dwelling on them. Apply the process laid out for us in Ephesians 4:22–24, which we looked at in Chapter 3:

Put Off Sinful Thoughts

Do not allow a fleeting image or thought to simmer in your mind. Choose to redirect your thoughts toward things that are pure.

Renew Your Mind

Use Scripture to replace the world's lies with truth, such as:

- The lusts of the flesh are deceitful and promise what they cannot deliver (Ephesians 4:22).
- This thought does not glorify or honor God (1 Corinthians 10:31).
- I *can* control my thinking, even when it is difficult (Philippians 4:8).
- Jesus suffered tremendously on the cross to forgive my sin of indulging my lust through pornography (Ephesians 1:7).
- Jesus sets me free from slavery to this sin and makes me a servant of God (Romans 6:6–7, 18).
- Dwelling on these thoughts is a waste of the valuable time God has given to me (Ephesians 5:15–17).

Find some other Scriptures that are meaningful to you and your struggle. Write them on 3x5 cards and carry them with you to review as needed. The goal here is to renew your mind in a positive way: focus on the grace of God and the help that he offers you. God's grace motivates us to surrender fleshly desires and pursue righteousness.

Put On Pure Thoughts

Focus your mind (and your body) on things that are meaningful and profitable. Make a list of fifteen things you can do to refocus when temptation comes. Be practical. Here are some ideas:

- Listen to Christian music or teaching.
- Pray for others or yourself.
- Watch a Bible-teaching program.
- Work on a task that you need to accomplish.
- Do your Bible study.

Cultivate Self-Control/Discipline

Self-control is a tremendous blessing, and yet many of us do not exercise it. We act impulsively, making decisions based on how we feel at the time. Living by our feelings feeds self-indulgence. It complicates our already complex lives. Living with self-control is the opposite of living by our feelings. A basic definition of what it means to live with self-control is *think before acting*.[17]

17 Edward T. Welch, *Addictions: A Banquet in the Grave* (Phillipsburg, NJ: P & R, 2001), 210.

Temptation to sin is strong, but God's Spirit is stronger. If you are truly born again, you *can* choose to do what is right. Before you choose to pick up that book, listen to that song, look at that video, or indulge in a daydream, *think!*

» Consider the possible consequences and whether or not it pleases the Lord.

» Think about what you have learned from past choices, both positive and negative.

» Examine how you may be trying to justify a wrong decision.

» After considering these things, *then* act. Make a decision to do what glorifies God. His glory is to be your motivation: "Therefore we also have as our ambition ... to be pleasing to Him" (2 Corinthians 5:9).

Observe when self-control is most difficult for you and then come up with a concrete plan to tackle such times. Make it easier to do what pleases God, and harder to sin.

» Keep a journal in which you record when you are most frequently tempted to indulge in your sin.

» Record the day, time, and what was happening during that time.
» Look for patterns (highlight them) so you can prepare for possible tempting times in advance.
» Write out several practical ideas you will start implementing during those tempting times.

Driving gave an opportunity for temptation for Denise. She had no radio in her car and it was quiet. Quiet time meant free time for her mind. To fill her mind with pure thoughts, she kept a portable radio with a tape player in her car. She listened to sermon tapes while driving, which focused her mind on the things of God. Listening to good Christian music was another option for her.

Cultivate Contentment and Gratitude

Ingratitude is a form of pride and self-pity. Pride proclaims, "You deserve good things, and you should be the one to determine what is good for you." Self-pity whispers, "Life hasn't been fair to you. God hasn't been fair! He is withholding from you that which is good."

Let's apply this to the issue of pornography.

Heather feels sorry for herself because she is not married. She is a Christian, and knows that sex is to be reserved for marriage. But she believes that God is withholding something good from her because she is not married and, therefore, does not get to experience sexual intimacy. Instead of obeying God's command to give thanks *in* all things and *for* all things (her singleness), Heather pities herself. She is not using singleness to serve the Lord without distractions. She tries to fulfill her physical desires and comfort herself by escaping into a fantasy world, submerging herself in steamy romance novels and masturbation. Heather has decided that God is holding out on her, and she has come up with a way to get what she wants. The same pattern can occur with a married woman who is not thankful or content with her husband.

If you want to learn contentment, start developing an attitude of gratitude:

» Begin a thanksgiving journal. Choose the very thing that you find it hard to be thankful for, and list ten ways you can give thanks *in* and *for* that situation (see Ephesians 5:20; 1 Thessalonians 5:18). Add five items to the list every day.

- Thank God for the position he has placed you in—indeed, *entrusted* you with—whether you are single or married.
- Paul says a lot about this subject in 1 Corinthians 7. Whatever state you are in, it is a gift from God. Have you considered this? Do your attitudes and thoughts reflect such a belief? Are you using your "gift" to serve the Lord?
- Examine what you think you deserve: A husband? A different husband? One who is ... does ... is not ... does not ...? Sexual pleasure? Bring these things before the Lord in confession and repentance.
- Take captive any thought that veers off into the corridors of ingratitude. (See "Cultivate Purity" above.) Replace those thoughts with truth (God's Word); choose to believe that our good and wise God knows what is best for you (Psalm 119:68).

Cultivate Honesty

Sin thrives in the dark. Deception strives to keep it there. Pornography is a "secret sin," often covered up with deception and lies in order to remain so. Over time, the habit of lying spills over to other areas of life. In your lies, you may be able to fool yourself and others, but you cannot fool God. He knows all about your secret sins *as well as* the ones that are more obvious. Bring them all into the light.

Do you find yourself hiding information, sneaking, blaming, manipulating others, changing the subject, rationalizing your behavior, or saying you will do something but not following through with it? These are all forms of deception. It's time to start being truthful with yourself, with others, and with God.

Be Honest With Yourself

» How do your private life and thoughts differ from what others see or think about you?

» In private, what do you do that you would not want anyone to know about?

Be Honest With Others

Utilize your local church. God designed the church to function as a body, with everyone operating together (1 Corinthians 12). One way we grow in Christlikeness is through accountability relationships within the church. Let's be honest with one other about our struggles. Pretending that we have it all together is not beneficial for anyone; we *all* struggle with sins and failures. We need our church family to encourage us in the truth and help us grow in love for God and others.

> *... [L]et us consider how to stimulate one another to love and good deeds, not forsaking our own assembling together, as is the habit of some, but encouraging one another ...*
>
> (Hebrews 10:24–25)

- » Find a godly woman in your church in whom you can confide about your struggle. Choose someone who will speak the truth to you in love, rather than allowing you to justify your sin (Ephesians 4:15).
- » Humble yourself and be open and honest with her.
- » Share with her your plan to break free from bondage to your sin.
- » Allow her to ask difficult, straightforward questions without becoming defensive toward her.
- » Be transparent without sharing too many

details. Talk openly with her about your struggles as well as your victories.

» Ask her to pray with you and hold you accountable to following your plan. Enlist her help to modify the plan as necessary.

» Contact her daily (five–ten minutes) for the first month, and then weekly.

Be Honest With God

» Confess your sin to God. He knows all about it already, but his mercy comes when you confess and forsake sin (Proverbs 28:13).

» Be specific, naming the sins you are guilty of (pornography, impure thoughts, masturbation, deceit, etc.). "If we confess our sins, He is faithful and righteous to forgive us our sins and to cleanse us from all unrighteousness" (1 John 1:9).

The fact that you are reading this booklet is commendable. But neither forgiveness nor lasting change will occur until you take your sin to the One who has the power to forgive and cleanse you of it (Psalm 130:4; Isaiah 43:25).

Conclusion: Continue in God's Grace

We are saved by the grace of God, and we are to live by the grace of God. When our sins seem abundant, we must remember that God's grace is *far more* abundant (Romans 5:20). We must allow his grace to overwhelm our minds, rather than dwelling on our sins and failures. Remember Romans 8:1:

> *Therefore there is now no condemnation for those who are in Christ Jesus.*

Rather than condemning those whose hearts are repentant, Jesus frees them (see John 8:1–11).

According to God, overcoming slavery to sin depends upon *grace*.

» God's grace saves us from the penalty of sin. "[E]ven when we were dead in our transgressions, [God] made us alive together with Christ ... For by grace you have been saved through faith; and that not of yourselves, it is the gift of God" (Ephesians 2:5a, 8).

» God's grace frees us from the power of sin; it changes us. "For the grace of God has appeared, bringing salvation to all men, instructing us to deny ungodliness and worldly desires and to live sensibly, righteously and godly in the present age" (Titus 2:11–12).

» God's grace is unlimited. It is not based on our deeds, but on Jesus' sacrifice on our behalf. "In [Jesus] we have redmption through His blood, the forgiveness of our trespasses, according to the riches of His grace which He lavished on us" (Ephesians 1:7–8a).

» God's grace motivates us to please him. "Or do you think lightly of the riches of His kindness and tolerance and patience, not knowing that *the kindness of God leads you to repentance*?" (Romans 2:4, emphasis added).

» We are responsible for seeking God's guidance through the Bible, but only God can give us the desire to please him and cause us to love him more. "[F]or it is God who is at work in

> you, both to will and to work for His good pleasure" (Philippians 2:13).

What if I Fail?

If you focus on a failure, you will find it easy to become discouraged and feel defeated. Such self-condemnation does not motivate you to change; God's grace does! Instead of focusing on what you have done wrong, ask the Lord to forgive you and then walk in his forgiveness. Turn your thoughts toward the riches of God's grace, because of Jesus' sacrifice for you. When you realize how great God's love and grace are toward *you personally*, you will love him more (see Luke 7:47). That love is what motivates you to live in a way that honors him, fulfilling the purpose and meaning of life.

> *Now to Him who is able to keep you from stumbling, and to make you stand in the presence of His glory blameless with great joy, to the only God our Savior, through Jesus Christ our Lord, be glory, majesty, dominion and authority, before all time and now and forever. Amen.*
>
> (Jude 24–25)

Personal Application Projects

These application projects are designed for women who are struggling with pornography. If you are seeking to help a woman with this struggle, encourage her to work through these projects.

Use a notebook or journal to complete the following projects. Remember to be honest with yourself and be as specific as possible with your answers.

Project 1: Personal Examination

1. *Over the next three to five weeks, consider what you allow into your mind through music, television, literature, the Internet, and so on. What do you need to put aside? Write out each specific item, including titles and/ or genres.*

2. *Write out what you will do right now to make it difficult to sin (Hebrews 12:1; Romans 13:14).*

Be practical (e.g. throw away ... [list book/magazine/movie/CD]; cancel cable).

Project 2: Motivation

1. *List each area that is a struggle for you (see Project 1), and what you think it gives you that makes you go back for more.*
2. *How did your involvement with pornography begin? With masturbation? Write it out.*
3. *What do you think led you to continue with it?*
4. Keep a record of tempting times. On a sheet of paper, create five columns:

    (a) Record the day and time of temptation.
    (b) Record what you were tempted to do (specifically).
    (c) Record where you were and whom you were with.
    (d) Record what you were thinking and doing just before becoming tempted.
    (e) Record what you actually did.

5. Highlight patterns to help you recognize what motivates you to pursue sexual sin—what

makes you return to it again (e.g. loneliness, boredom, pleasure).

6. Brainstorm at least five practical, God-honoring ways to handle each potentially tempting situation.

Project 3: Genuine Repentance

1. Read 2 Corinthians 7:9–10. What two types of sorrow are identified here, and how can a person tell the difference? What kind of sorrow have you experienced over your sin? How do you know?
2. Look at 1 Thessalonians 1:9 and Proverbs 28:13, both of which describe what repentance looks like. How do these verses "picture" repentance? Does your life illustrate true repentance? Why or why not?

Project 4: The Grace of God

1. Look up the following passages and mark every occurrence of the word "grace" in a distinctive way. List everything you learn about grace (what it is, what it does, the purpose of grace, who gives and receives grace, etc.): John 1:14–17; Romans 5–6, 11:1–6;

1 Corinthians 15:1–10; 2 Corinthians 9:8; 12:7–10; Ephesians 1:2–8; 2:1–10; 2 Thessalonians 2:16–17; 1 Timothy 1:12–17; Titus 2:11–14; Hebrews 4:15–16.

2. *How will God's grace help you in the battle against pornography? What lessons and encouragement have you received from his Word?*

Where Can I Get More Help?

Adams, Jay E., *What Do You Do When You Know that You're Hooked?* (Phillipsburg, NJ: P & R, 1992)

Arthur, Kay, *The Truth About Sex* (Colorado Springs: WaterBrook Press, 2005)

Cleveland, Mike, *The Way of Purity: Enjoy Lasting Freedom in Christ* (Bemidji, MN: Focus, 2007)

Covenant Eyes Internet filter and accountability: www.covenanteyes.com

Coyle, Rachel, "The Taboo Topic: Pornography and Women," ch. 22 in Fitzpatrick, Elyse, (ed.), *Women Counseling Women: Biblical Answers to Life's Difficult Problems* (Eugene, OR: Harvest House, 2010)

DeMoss, Nancy Leigh, *Becoming a Woman of Discretion in a Sensual World* (Buchanan, MI: Life Action Ministries, 2003)

Fitzpatrick, Elyse, *Idols of the Heart: Learning to Long for God Alone* (Phillipsburg, NJ: P & R, 2001)

Setting Captives Free Ministry: www.settingcaptivesfree.com

Vandegriff, John, *In the Arena of the Mind* (Howell, NJ: Ask, Seek, Knock Publishing, 1992)

Welch, Edward T., *Addictions: A Banquet in the Grave* (Phillipsburg, NJ: P & R, 2001)